D1794791

Dip into Hummus

Discover 40 Must-Make Hummus Recipes
Today!

BY

Christina Tosch

Copyright Notes

vvvvvvvvvvvvvvvvvvvvvvvvvvvvvvvvvvvvvvvvvvvvvvvvvvvv

A special thank you for purchasing my book!

My sincerest thanks for purchasing my book! As added thanks, you are now eligible to receive a complimentary book sent to your email every week. To get started on this exclusive offer, fill in the box below by entering your email address and start receiving notifications of special promotions. It's not every day you get something for free for doing so little! Free and discounted books are available every day and a reminder will be sent to you so you never have to miss out. Fill in the box below and get started on this amazing offer!

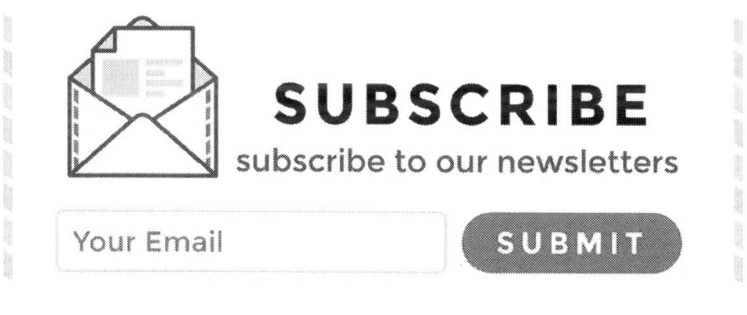

https://christina.subscribemenow.com

Table of Contents

vv

Introduction

Traditionally made with chickpeas (aka garbanzo beans), tahini, olive oil, garlic, fresh lemon juice, and garlic, hummus is a food staple in Israel, Egypt, Turkey, Syria, Palestine, Cyprus, and Jordan.

Its popularity as a dip, spread or meze has now extended to the Western world, and while its preparation may differ from country to country, its basic ingredients stay the same.

So, let's dip into some interesting hummus facts!

- The earliest mention of hummus dates back to Egypt and the 13th century

- Hummus is low in saturated fat and high in both protein and fiber
- The word hummus derives from the Arabic word for chickpeas
- A staggering 25 percent of Americans stock hummus in their refrigerators
- Many believe hummus to be an aphrodisiac, thanks mainly to the fact that chickpeas contain an amino acid responsible for increasing blood circulation
- The writings of Ancient Greek philosophers Socrates and Plato have both made references to the nutritional value of hummus
- Natalie Portman follows a plant-based diet and claims to consume her body weight in hummus every day!
- International Hummus Day takes place every year on May 13
- In March 2016, competitive eater, American Matt Stonie ate over 5 pounds of hummus in just 6 minutes. Now that's what we call a big dipper!

vvvvvvvvvvvvvvvvvvvvvvvvvvvvvvvvvvvvvvvvvvvvvvvvvvvvv

Hummus

vvvvvvvvvvvvvvvvvvvvvvvvvvvvvvvvvvvvvvvvvvvvvvvvvvvv

Green Pea Hummus

Colorful, and flavorful this fresh from the garden pea hummus is the perfect party dip.

Servings: 10

Total Prep Time: 10mins

Ingredients:

- 1 (15 ounce) can chickpeas (un-drained)
- 1 cup fresh garden peas
- 2 tbsp tahini
- 2 tsp freshly squeezed lemon juice
- 1 garlic clove (peeled, minced)
- Pinch of salt
- Dash of black pepper

Directions:

1. Over a bowl, drain the chickpeas. Set the liquid (aquafaba) to one side.

2. Add the peas to a food blender together with the tahini, fresh lemon juice, garlic, salt, and black pepper. Add 4 tbsp of the chickpea liquid.

3. Process the mixture for 2-3 minutes, until creamy and thick. Scrape the sides of the blender down and add additional aquafaba if needed, and until you achieve your preferred consistency.

4. Serve and enjoy.

vvvvvvvvvvvvvvvvvvvvvvvvvvvvvvvvvvvvvvvvvvvvvvvvvv

Carrot Hummus

Beta-carotene-rich, sweet carrots add a new dimension to creamy hummus.

Servings: 16

Total Prep Time: 1hour 15mins

Ingredients:

- 1 cup carrots (chopped)
- 1 (15 ounce) can chickpeas (rinsed, drained)
- ¼ cup tahini
- 2 tbsp freshly squeezed lemon juice
- 2 garlic cloves (peeled, quartered)
- ½ tsp ground cumin
- ¼ tsp salt
- 2 tbsp fresh parsley (snipped)

Directions:

1. In a small pan with lid, cook the carrots in a boiling water for 6-8 minutes, until fork tender. Drain.

2. In a food processor combine the drained carrots with the chickpeas, tahini, fresh lemon juice, garlic, cumin, and salt. Cover with a lid and process until the mixture is creamy smooth.

3. Transfer the hummus to a bowl and fold in the snipped parsley.

4. Cover with kitchen wrap, and chill in the fridge for 60 minutes before serving.

vvvvvvvvvvvvvvvvvvvvvvvvvvvvvvvvvvvvvvvvvvvvvvvvvvvvv

Artichoke Hummus

A healthy chickpea and artichoke hummus make for a great snack or perfect appetizer. It's colorful, flavorful, and easy to make.

Servings: 6-8

Total Prep Time: 12mins

Ingredients:

- 15 ounces chickpeas (drained, rinsed)
- 6 ounces marinated artichoke hearts (drained, rinsed)
- 1 garlic clove (peeled, chopped)
- 2 tbsp tahini
- Freshly squeezed juice of ½ lemon
- 2 tbsp extra-virgin olive oil
- ¼ cup water
- ½ tsp kosher salt
- Sriracha (to taste)
- Olive oil (to drizzle)

Directions:

1. In a food blender or processor, combine the chickpeas with the artichoke hearts, garlic, tahini, fresh lemon juice, and oil. Process until a smooth consistency, adding water to thin as needed.

2. Add salt and Sriracha to taste along with additional lemon juice or tahini, if needed.

3. Spoon the hummus onto a serving plate, make a shallow well in the middle and drizzle with olive oil.

4. Serve with your favorite chips.

vvvvvvvvvvvvvvvvvvvvvvvvvvvvvvvvvvvvvvvvvvvvvvvvvv

Basil Hummus

Bring out your inner green god or goddess with this vibrant hummus dip, to share.

Servings: 8-10

Total Prep Time: 12mins

Ingredients:

- ¼ cup pine nuts
- 2 cups packed sweet basil leaves
- 3 garlic cloves (peeled, smashed, minced)
- 2 (15 ounce) cans chickpeas (rinsed, drained)
- ¼ cup olive oil
- ⅓ cup freshly squeezed lemon juice
- 1½ -2 tsp salt
- 1 tsp tomato paste
- Tabasco (as needed)
- ¼ cup water (as needed)

Directions:

1. First, toast the pine nuts. In a skillet on moderate high heat, heat the nuts, stirring as they begin to lightly brown.

2. When the majority of the nuts are gently browned, remove them from the skillet and transfer to a bowl to cool. Set aside a spoonful of nuts to use as a garnish later.

3. Using a food processor, pulse the basil leaves along with the garlic until finely chopped.

4. Add the chickpeas, along with the pine nuts, oil, fresh lemon juice, salt, tomato paste, and Tabasco (to taste). Pulse for 5-6 seconds each time, until the mixture is smooth. Taste, and add additional salt, Tabasco or fresh lemon, as needed.

5. A little at a time add the water until you achieve your preferred consistency.

6. When you are ready to serve, drizzle with oil and garnish with the toasted nuts set aside earlier.

vvvvvvvvvvvvvvvvvvvvvvvvvvvvvvvvvvvvvvvvvvvvvvvvvvvv

Spicy Orange Hummus

Dip-in to this unique artisanal hummus with its zesty citrus notes and hot spices.

Servings: 16-20

Total Prep Time: 25mins

Ingredients:

- 2 (10½ ounce) cans chickpeas (rinsed, drained)
- ½ cup olive oil
- Rind of 3 large-size oranges (finely grated)
- ½ cup freshly squeezed orange
- 2 tbsp tahini
- 4 cloves of garlic (peeled, crushed)
- 2 tsp ground cumin
- ¼-½ tsp cayenne pepper (to taste)
- Salt and freshly ground black pepper
- Small fresh coriander leaves (to serve)

Directions:

1. Add the chickpeas, oil, orange rind, along with a ½ cup of fresh orange, tahini, garlic, cumin and ¼ tsp of cayenne pepper to a food processor, and process to a smooth consistency.

2. Taste and season with salt, pepper, and remaining cayenne.

3. Garnish with coriander leaves, serve with pita and enjoy

vvvvvvvvvvvvvvvvvvvvvvvvvvvvvvvvvvvvvvvvvvvvvvvvvv

Beer Hummus

Game night in? Then this beer hummus will get the perfect score. Serve with fresh bread or potato chips.

Servings: 10-12

Total Prep Time: 10mins

Ingredients:

- 2 (15½ ounce) cans chickpeas (drained)
- 1 tsp freshly squeezed lemon juice
- 2 garlic cloves (peeled, minced)
- 1 tsp sesame seeds
- ¼ cup India pale ale
- 1 tsp coriander
- 1 tsp cumin
- ½ tsp salt
- ¼ tsp cayenne
- Fresh bread

Directions:

1. Add all of the ingredients in recipe order (chickpeas, lemon juice, garlic, sesame seeds, pale ale, coriander, cumin, salt, and cayenne) to a food processor and blend to a smooth consistency.

2. Serve with fresh bread and enjoy.

vvvvvvvvvvvvvvvvvvvvvvvvvvvvvvvvvvvvvvvvvvvvvvvvvv

Turmeric Hummus

Not only do turmeric and paprika add color to this creamy dip, but also both spices have lots of important health benefits. Turmeric has anti-inflammatory properties and is excellent for the skin while paprika helps to improve indigestion and circulation.

Servings: 8

Total Prep Time: 8mins

Ingredients:

- 15 ounces canned chickpeas (drained)
- ½ cup canned chickpea liquid (divided, as needed)
- ½ cup olive oil
- 1 tsp sesame oil
- ⅓ cup freshly squeezed lemon juice
- 4 tsp garlic (peeled, minced)
- 2 tsp paprika
- 2 tsp turmeric
- ¾ tsp salt
- ¼ tsp black pepper

Directions:

1. Add the drained chickpeas, a ¼ cup of chickpea liquid, olive oil, sesame oil, fresh lemon juice, minced garlic, paprika, turmeric, salt and black pepper to a food blender and process for 60 seconds.

2. Add some additional chickpea liquid if needed to get your preferred consistency.

3. Dip and enjoy.

vvvvvvvvvvvvvvvvvvvvvvvvvvvvvvvvvvvvvvvvvvvvvvvvvv

Browned Butter Maple Hummus

Next time you get an attack of the munchies serve this sweet hummus with fresh fruit or crisp rice cakes.

Servings: 6-8

Total Prep Time: 15mins

Ingredients:

- 1 cup canned chickpeas (drained, rinsed)
- ¼ cup tahini
- ¼ cup maple syrup
- 2 tbsp butter
- ½ tsp vanilla essence
- ¼ tsp cinnamon
- 2-3 pinches of fresh nutmeg
- Salt (to taste)

Directions:

1. Add the chickpeas along with the tahini and maple syrup to a food blender or processor and on the pulse setting, combine.

2. Over moderate heat, cook the butter in a pan until it gently browns and emits its nutty fragrance.

3. While the processor is running, drizzle in the butter.

4. Turn the processor off, scrape down the sides and add the vanilla essence, cinnamon, nutmeg and a pinch of salt, to taste. Process until creamy smooth.

5. Serve with fresh fruit or rice cakes.

vvvvvvvvvvvvvvvvvvvvvvvvvvvvvvvvvvvvvvvvvvvvvvvvv

Cajun Hummus

This Mediterranean classic gets a hot and spicy makeover.

Servings: 8

Total Prep Time: 6mins

Ingredients:

- 1 (14 ounce) can chickpeas (drained, rinsed)
- ¼ cup olive oil
- 3 cloves garlic (peeled)
- 2 tbsp freshly squeezed lemon juice
- 2 tbsp tahini
- 1-2 tbsp. cayenne pepper (to taste)
- 2 tsp paprika
- 1 tsp dried thyme
- ½ tsp freshly ground black pepper
- ¼ tsp salt
- 1-2 scallions (chopped)
- Dash of hot sauce (to serve)

Directions:

1. Add the chickpeas, oil, garlic, lemon juice, tahini, cayenne pepper, paprika, dried thyme, black pepper, and salt to the bowl of your processor, and blend until combined and creamy smooth.

2. Transfer to a dish, garnish with scallions and a dash of hot sauce and serve.

vvvvvvvvvvvvvvvvvvvvvvvvvvvvvvvvvvvvvvvvvvvvvvvvv

Chipotle Hummus

Whip up a batch of this spicy hummus in just 10 minutes, pop it in the fridge for up to two weeks and serve as needed. What could be simpler?

Servings: 10-12

Total Prep Time: 10mins

Ingredients:

- 1½ cups chickpeas (cooked, rinsed, drained)
- 2 tbsp freshly squeezed lemon juice
- ½ cup water
- ¼ cup tahini
- 1 tsp sea salt
- 1 tsp onion powder
- 1 large-sized garlic clove (peeled)
- ¼ tsp chipotle powder

Directions:

1. Add the chickpeas, lemon juice, water, tahini, sea salt, onion powder, garlic and chipotle powder to a food processor, and blend to a creamy consistency.

2. Add additional water to thin out as necessary.

3. Store in the fridge for up to 14 days.

vvvvvvvvvvvvvvvvvvvvvvvvvvvvvvvvvvvvvvvvvvvvvvvvv

Fried Rosemary Hummus

Crisp and delicious this rosemary infused hummus will have everyone chipping n' dipping.

Servings: 6-8

Total Prep Time: 5mins

Ingredients:

- 2½ tbsp olive oil
- 3-4 sprigs of fresh rosemary
- 2 (15 ounce) cans chickpeas (drained)
- ⅓ cup plain Greek yogurt
- 1 tsp freshly squeezed lemon juice
- 1 large-sized garlic clove (peeled)
- 1 tsp salt
- Black pepper

Directions:

1. Over high heat, heat the oil in a skillet until smoking.

2. Add the sprigs of rosemary and flash fry on each side for 30 seconds.

3. Remove the rosemary from the skillet and place on a plate lined with kitchen paper towel. Reserve the olive oil.

4. Add the chickpeas to a food processor along with the Greek yogurt, rosemary oil (set aside earlier) fresh lemon juice, garlic, salt, and black pepper. Puree to your preferred consistency.

5. Carefully remove the crisp rosemary leaves from the stems and add to the processor. Pulse until incorporated.

6. Serve and enjoy.

vvvvvvvvvvvvvvvvvvvvvvvvvvvvvvvvvvvvvvvvvvvvvvvvvvvvv

Greek Yogurt Hummus

The secret ingredient to this Greek hummus is creamy yogurt. Serve with cucumber sticks and enjoy.

Servings: 6

Total Prep Time: 7mins

Ingredients:

- 1 garlic clove (peeled)
- 1 (15 ounce) can chickpeas
- ½ cup plain Greek yogurt
- 1 tbsp water
- ½ tsp salt
- 1 tsp freshly squeezed lemon juice

Directions:

1. Add the garlic along with the chickpeas to the Greek yogurt, water, salt and lemon juice to a food processor, and pulse until smooth.

vvvvvvvvvvvvvvvvvvvvvvvvvvvvvvvvvvvvvvvvvvvvvvvvvv

Harissa Hummus

North African hot chili pepper paste or harissa certainly hots up a bowl of hummus!

Servings: 6

Total Prep Time: 10mins

Ingredients:

- 3 garlic cloves (peeled)
- 2 cups canned chickpeas (drained, liquid reserved*)
- 1½ tsp salt
- ¼ cup tahini
- 5 tbsp freshly squeezed lemon juice
- 2 tbsp chickpea liquid*
- 1½ tbsp harissa
- Pita (to serve)

Directions:

1. Switch on your food blender, and through the hole in the lid, add the garlic, processing until minced.

2. Add the remaining ingredients (chickpeas, salt, tahini, lemon juice, chickpea liquid, and harissa), and process until a smooth consistency. Transfer to a bowl.

3. Serve and enjoy with pita.

vvvvvvvvvvvvvvvvvvvvvvvvvvvvvvvvvvvvvvvvvvvvvvvvvvv

Hazelnut Hummus

A nutty, flavorful hummus to enjoy as a spread or dip.

Servings: 6

Total Prep Time: 20mins

Ingredients:

- ¼ cup hazelnut butter
- 1 (14 ounce) can chickpeas (drained, rinsed)
- 3 tbsp extra-virgin olive oil
- 1 clove garlic (peeled, chopped)
- 1 tbsp parsley (chopped)
- 2 tbsp freshly squeezed lemon juice
- Salt and pepper
- 1 tbsp hazelnut oil

Directions:

1. In a food processor, combine the hazelnut butter with the chickpeas, oil, garlic, parsley, and fresh lemon juice and process to a smooth consistency.

2. One tablespoon at a time add water until you achieve your desired consistency.

3. Season to taste with salt and pepper and drizzle with hazelnut oil before serving.

vvvvvvvvvvvvvvvvvvvvvvvvvvvvvvvvvvvvvvvvvvvvvvvvvvvv

Horseradish Hummus

Creamy hummus with a horseradish kick is sure to tick the taste boxes.

Servings: 6

Total Prep Time: 1hour 5mins

Ingredients:

- 1 (15½ ounce) can chickpeas (drained, rinsed)
- 1 garlic clove (peeled, minced)
- 2 tbsp freshly squeezed lemon juice
- 1 tbsp tahini
- 2 tbsp ready-made horseradish
- ¼ cup extra-virgin olive oil
- Freshly ground black pepper (to taste)

Directions:

1. Add all ingredients (garlic, chickpeas, tahini, lemon juice, horseradish, oil, and black pepper to taste to the bowl of your food processor and process until smooth, creamy and combined.

2. Place in the fridge for 1-2 hours to chill.

3. Enjoy.

vvvvvvvvvvvvvvvvvvvvvvvvvvvvvvvvvvvvvvvvvvvvvvvvvvvvvvv

Lemon Hummus

This light and fresh hummus dip pairs well with crackers, pita or veggie batons, and what's more, it's easy to make.

Servings: 8-10

Total Prep Time: 20mins

Ingredients:

- 2 (15½ ounce) cans chickpeas
- ¼ cup tahini
- ¼ cup freshly squeezed lemon juice
- 1 tbsp lemon zest
- ½ tsp kosher salt
- ¼ cup extra-virgin olive oil
- Olive oil (to serve)

Directions:

1. First, drain and rinse the chickpeas

2. Pinch the chickpeas to remove their skins.

3. In the bowl of a food processor, combine the peeled chickpeas with the tahini, fresh lemon juice, lemon zest, and kosher salt. Process for 5-7 minutes, until a puree consistency. While the processor is still running gradually drizzle in the oil until combined.

4. When you are ready to serve, drizzle with olive oil.

vvvvvvvvvvvvvvvvvvvvvvvvvvvvvvvvvvvvvvvvvvvvvvvvvvvv

Mushroom Hummus

The earthy flavor of mushrooms lends itself perfectly to creamy hummus while a hint of fresh lemon juice adds a welcome citrus twist.

Servings: 6-8

Total Prep Time: 25mins

Ingredients:

- 3 cups baby Bella mushrooms (sliced)
- ¼-½ cup + 2 tbsp olive oil
- Sea salt and freshly cracked pepper
- 1 (14 ounce) can chickpeas (drained, liquid reserved)
- ⅓ cup tahini
- 2 garlic cloves (peeled)
- Freshly squeezed juice of 1 lemon
- 1 tbsp parsley (chopped)

Directions:

1. Preheat the main oven to 425 degrees F.

2. Arrange the sliced mushrooms on a baking tray, drizzle the mushrooms with 2 tbsp of oil and season with salt and black pepper. Roast in the preheated oven until browned, for 15 minutes. Stir the mushrooms half-way through roasting.

3. Remove the mushrooms out of the oven and set to one side.

4. In a food processor, combine a ¼ cup of oil with the chickpeas, tahini, garlic, and fresh lemon juice and on pulse, process for 2-3 seconds. Add additional oil, as needed.

5. Add the mushrooms to the processor and pulse.

6. Add sufficient of the chickpea liquid to the mixture until you achieve your preferred consistency.

7. Season to taste and serve.

Pineapple Hummus with Smoked Paprika

Mediterranean hummus gets a tropical twist with canned, crushed pineapple while smoked paprika adds a spicy kick.

Servings: 10-12

Total Prep Time: 40mins

Ingredients:

- 2 cloves garlic (peeled)
- 1 (8 ounce) can crushed pineapple (drained)
- 2 Serrano peppers (seeded)
- ½ cup tahini
- 1 (15 ounce) can chickpeas (un-drained)
- ½ tsp bicarbonate of soda
- 2 tbsp olive oil
- Freshly squeezed juice of 1 lemon
- 1 tsp smoked paprika
- 1 tsp sea salt
- Sesame seeds (to garnish)
- Smoked paprika (to garnish)

Directions:

1. In a food processor or blender add the garlic along with the pineapple, Serrano pepper, and tahini. Pulse to combine and roughly chop.

2. In a pan over moderate heat, add the chickpeas along with their liquid, the bicarbonate of soda, and sufficient water to cover the beans by ½".

3. Bring to the mixture to boil and cook until the chickpeas are softened, for 5 minutes.

4. Remove the pan from the heat and rinse with hot water.

5. Add the rinsed beans to the food processor and on pulse, combine until nearly mixed.

6. Add 1-2 tbsp of hot water, and once again pulse, until creamy. Scrape down the sides of the bowl as needed.

7. Next, add the oil, fresh lemon juice, and smoked paprika and pulse to incorporate. Season to taste with salt.

8. Remove from the food processor and place in the fridge to chill for 15 minutes.

9. When you are ready to serve, sprinkle with sesame seeds, additional paprika and a light drizzle of olive oil.

10. Serve with bagel chips or pita.

vvvvvvvvvvvvvvvvvvvvvvvvvvvvvvvvvvvvvvvvvvvvvvvvvvv

Pistachio Hummus

Great for snacking, this nutty, fragrant hummus is bursting with flavor.

Servings: 8-10

Total Prep Time: 10mins

Ingredients:

- 1 (15 ounce) can chickpeas (drained, liquid reserved)
- 2 garlic cloves (peeled)
- 2 tbsp fresh parsley
- 2 tbsp tahini
- 1 tsp extra virgin olive oil
- 2 tbsp freshly squeezed lemon juice
- Sea salt and black pepper
- ½ cup shelled pistachios
- Shelled pistachios (to garnish)
- Pita (to serve, optional)

Directions:

1. Combine the chickpeas, garlic, parsley, tahini, oil, fresh lemon juice, salt, black pepper and pistachios to a food processor and puree. Add the chickpea liquid, a little at a time until you achieve your preferred consistency. Scrape down the sides of the bowl as necessary.

2. Transfer to a serving bowl, garnish with pistachios and enjoy with wedges of pita.

vvvvvvvvvvvvvvvvvvvvvvvvvvvvvvvvvvvvvvvvvvvvvvvvv

Pomegranate Hummus

This posh party hummus is sure to take pride of place at your next get together.

Servings: 4-6

Total Prep Time: 1hour 20mins

Ingredients:

- ½ cup raw chickpeas
- 1 tsp baking soda (divided)
- ½ cup pomegranate juice
- ¼ cup sugar
- 3 cups water
- Freshly squeezed juice of 1 lemon
- ¼ cup tahini
- 2 garlic cloves (peeled, finely minced)
- ½ tsp ground cumin
- 2 tbsp extra-virgin olive oil
- 3 tbsp chickpea liquid*
- Salt and black pepper
- ¼ cup pomegranate arils

Directions:

1. The evening before you wish to prepare the hummus, add a ½ cup of chickpeas and ½ tsp of baking soda to a large bowl. Cover with cold water and soak overnight to double in size.

2. The following day and in a pan, combine the pomegranate juice with the sugar and bring to a low simmer, Simmer, while occasionally stirring for 15-20 minutes until the mixture is reduced to a quarter of the original amount. Set aside to cool and thicken.

3. Add the cooked, drained and rinsed chickpeas to a large pan with ½ tsp of baking powder and cook while continually stirring for a few minutes. Add sufficient cold water to cover the chickpeas by a 3-4" and bring to boil. Skim off any surface foam and cook for an additional 60 minutes, until the chickpeas are tender and beginning to fall apart.

4. Drain and set the cooking liquid to one side.

5. Add the drained chickpeas to a food processor and puree.

6. Add the lemon juice along with the tahini, garlic, cumin, oil and 1 tbsp of pomegranate syrup followed by 3 tbsp of chickpeas cooking liquid, set aside earlier. Puree and season to taste. You may need to add a drop more chickpea liquid if necessary, to achieve your preferred consistency.

7. Remove from the processor and serve drizzled with additional pomegranate syrup and garnish with arils.

vvvvvvvvvvvvvvvvvvvvvvvvvvvvvvvvvvvvvvvvvvvvvvvvvvv

Ranch Hummus Dip

Ranch dip mix adds bold flavor to traditional hummus.

Servings: 6

Total Prep Time: 5mins

Ingredients:

- 1 (15 ounce) can chickpeas (rinsed, drained)
- 1 cup fat-free cottage cheese
- ¼ cup non-fat Greek yogurt
- 1 (1 ounce) packet ranch dip mix
- 1 tbsp olive oil
- 1 tbsp freshly squeezed lemon juice

Directions:

1. In a food blender, combine the chickpeas, cottage cheese, Greek yogurt, ranch dip mix, olive oil, and fresh lemon juice. Puree until smooth.

2. Serve and enjoy.

Roasted Celery Hummus

Need a pick-me-up? Whip up a fresh batch of this roasted celery hummus. Serve with crisp sticks of celery and enjoy.

Servings: 2-4

Total Prep Time: 1hour

Ingredients:

- 1 cup celery (trimmed, cut into 1/3" pieces)
- 5 tbsp extra virgin olive oil (divided)
- 2 garlic cloves (peeled)
- 1 green Serrano chili (minced)
- 1 cup cooked chickpeas (drained, rinsed)
- ⅓ cup tahini
- 2 tbsp freshly squeezed lime juice
- 1 tsp salt
- 1 tbsp fresh parsley (minced)
- Celery sticks (to serve)

Directions:

1. Put the celery in a casserole dish and drizzle with 2 tbsp of oil.

2. Place the garlic cloves in opposite corners of the dish.

3. Scatter the minced chili over the top.

4. Bake in an oven set at 350 degrees F, for 45 minutes.

5. Remove from the oven and set aside to slightly cool.

6. Add the chickpeas to a food blender along with the celery and any residual oil.

7. Add the tahini followed by the fresh lime juice, salt, and process for 3-4 minutes, until smooth.

8. Remove from the food blender and stir in the remaining oil and minced parsley.

9. Serve with sticks of celery for dipping.

vvvvvvvvvvvvvvvvvvvvvvvvvvvvvvvvvvvvvvvvvvvvvvvvvvvvv

Roasted Fennel Hummus

Roasted fennel hummus has great flavor. Its licorice tones combine perfectly with fresh lemon juice to create the perfect dip or spread.

Servings: 8

Total Prep Time: 45mins

Ingredients:

- 1 medium fennel bulb (fronds removed, reserved)
- 1½ cups of cooked chickpeas (drained)
- ¼ cup extra-virgin olive oil
- 3 tbsp water
- 2 tbsp tahini paste
- 2 tbsp freshly squeezed lemon juice
- 2 cloves garlic (peeled)
- ½ tsp sea salt
- Fennel fronds (to garnish)

Directions:

1. Preheat the main oven to 400 degrees F.

2. Chop the fennel into quarters and on a baking sheet lined with parchment paper roast in the preheated oven until golden; this will take around half an hour.

3. In a processor, combine the chickpeas with the oil, water, tahini, fresh lemon juice, garlic, and sea salt. Process to a smooth consistency.

4. Add the roasted fennel and puree.

5. Taste, season, garnish with fennel fronds and serve with chips.

vvvvvvvvvvvvvvvvvvvvvvvvvvvvvvvvvvvvvvvvvvvvvvvvvv

Roasted Red Pepper Hummus

From food blender to bowl in less than 10 minutes. This dip has to be your next go-to snack.

Servings: 6

Total Prep Time: 8mins

Ingredients:

- 1 (14 ounce) can chickpeas (drained, liquid reserved*)
- ½ cup roasted red pepper (coarsely chopped)
- ¼ cup chickpea liquid*
- 1 tbsp freshly squeezed lemon juice
- 1 tbsp tahini
- 1 garlic clove (peeled)
- ⅛ tsp cumin
- Salt (to taste)

Directions:

1. Add all the ingredients to a food blender (chickpeas, red pepper, chickpea liquid, lemon juice, tahini, garlic, and cumin and process to a creamy smooth consistency. Taste and season with salt.

2. Transfer to the fridge for up to 4 days.

3. Serve with veggie batons, bagel chips or pita.

vvvvvvvvvvvvvvvvvvvvvvvvvvvvvvvvvvvvvvvvvvvvvvvvvv

Slow Roasted Tomato Hummus

Tangy slow roasted tomatoes make for a great tasting hummus. Serve with strips of fresh red pepper for a flavor sensation.

Servings: 6

Total Prep Time: 15mins

Ingredients:

- ½ cup slow roasted tomatoes
- 2 tbsp garlic puree
- 1 (15½ ounce) can chickpeas
- ¼ cup tahini sauce
- 2-3 tbsp freshly squeezed lemon juice
- 2 tbsp olive oil
- ¼ cup water
- ½ tsp sea salt
- Red peppers (cut into strips, to serve, optional)
- Crackers or pita (to serve, optional)

Directions:

1. Add the tomatoes to a food processor bowl along with the garlic puree and process for 30-40 seconds.

2. Add the drained chickpeas to the processor and process until combined, for 1-2 minutes.

3. Next, add the tahini followed by 2 tbsp of fresh lemon juice, oil, and half of the water. Process for 30-60 seconds, until the ingredients are fully incorporated.

4. Add additional water if needed.

5. Taste and add the remaining lemon juice, if necessary along with a pinch of salt. Process for a few more seconds.

6. Serve with strips of red pepper, crackers or pita.

vvvvvvvvvvvvvvvvvvvvvvvvvvvvvvvvvvvvvvvvvvvvvvvvvvvvv

Spicy Peach Barbecue Hummus

Four ingredients, and only five minutes to prepare! Wow, that's a real game changer.

Servings: 8

Total Prep Time: 5mins

Ingredients:

- 1 (15 ounce) can chickpeas (drained)
- ½ cup BBQ sauce
- ¼ cup peach preserves
- 2+ tsp chipotle hot sauce (to taste)
- Veggie batons (to serve)

Directions:

1. In a food blender, combine the chickpeas along with the BBQ sauce, peach preserves and hot sauce (to taste), and puree until a smooth consistency.

2. Taste and adjust the seasoning, as needed. To sweeten, add more peach preserves, and re-blend. To add heat, add more hot sauce and re-blend.

3. Transfer to the fridge to chill, until you are ready to serve.

vvvvvvvvvvvvvvvvvvvvvvvvvvvvvvvvvvvvvvvvvvvvvvvvvvvv

Spinach Hummus

It doesn't have to be International Hummus Day to enjoy this power-packed hummus dip.

Servings: 8-10

Total Prep Time: 5mins

Ingredients:

- 2 (14½ ounce) cans chickpeas (drained, liquid reserved*)
- 4 cups baby spinach leaves
- ⅔ cup tahini
- 6 tbsp freshly squeezed lemon juice
- 4 medium-sized garlic cloves (peeled, minced)
- 1 tsp salt
- 1 tsp cumin
- Chickpea liquid*
- Extra-virgin olive oil (to garnish)
- Paprika (to garnish)

Directions:

1. In a food blender, combine the drained chickpeas together with the baby spinach leaves, tahini, fresh lemon juice, minced garlic, salt, and cumin. On the pulse setting, process while gradually streaming in the chickpea liquid to create a creamy smooth hummus.

2. Season to taste, drizzle with oil and garnish with a sprinkling of paprika.

vvvvvvvvvvvvvvvvvvvvvvvvvvvvvvvvvvvvvvvvvvvvvv

Sunflower Seed Hummus

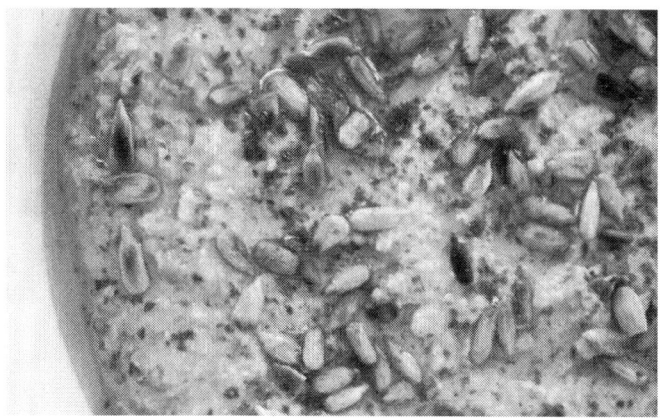

Sunflower seeds will not only make the hummus a thicker consistency than usual, but also they will give it a great nutty flavor.

Servings: 8

Total Prep Time: 10mins

Ingredients:

- 4 cloves of garlic (peeled)
- 1 cup sunflower seeds
- 2 (15½ ounce) cans chickpeas (drained, rinsed)
- Freshly squeezed juice of 1 lemon
- 1 tbsp extra-virgin olive oil
- 1 tsp salt
- ¼-⅓ cup water
- Sunflower seeds (to garnish)
- Veggie batons (to serve)

Directions:

1. To a food processor, add the garlic cloves, and mince.

2. Next, add the sunflower seeds to the processor and process until they are a meal-like consistency.

3. Add the rinsed chickpeas together with the freshly squeezed lemon juice, olive oil, salt and ¼ cup of water. Process, until you achieve your ideal consistency. You may need to add water, as necessary. The consistency of the hummus will be a little bit thicker than regular hummus due to the addition of sunflower seeds.

4. Transfer the hummus to a bowl and garnish with sunflower seeds.

5. Serve with veggie batons and enjoy.

vvvvvvvvvvvvvvvvvvvvvvvvvvvvvvvvvvvvvvvvvvvvvvvvvv

Thai Coconut Curry Hummus

If you are a fan of Asian flavors, then this spicy hummus is the one for you!

Servings: 8-10

Total Prep Time: 7mins

Ingredients:

- 2 (14½ ounce) cans chickpeas (drained)
- ⅓ cup Thai red curry paste
- 3 garlic cloves (peeled)
- Zest of 2 fresh limes
- 1 tsp sea salt
- ¾ cup unsweetened full-fat coconut milk
- Fresh Thai basil leaves (to garnish)
- Veggie batons or crackers (to serve, optional)

Directions:

1. Add the chickpeas, red curry paste, garlic, fresh lime zest, and sea salt to your food processor.

2. Pour in ½ cup of coconut milk, and process to a creamy puree. Add additional milk if needed to achieve your preferred consistency.

3. Transfer to a bowl and garnish with Thai basil leaves.

4. Serve with crackers or veggie batons.

vvvvvvvvvvvvvvvvvvvvvvvvvvvvvvvvvvvvvvvvvvvvvvvvv

Traditional Hummus with Lobster

Add freshly cooked lobster meat to a traditional hummus a dinner-party worth gourmet appetizer or dip.

Servings: 16

Total Prep Time: 10mins

Ingredients:

- 1½ cups chickpea liquid
- 1 cup ice cubes
- 5 (15½ ounce) cans chickpeas (drained, liquid reserved*)
- 8 cloves of garlic (peeled)
- 1 cup freshly squeezed lemon juice
- 4 tsp sea salt
- ¼ tsp cumin
- 3 tbsp tahini
- ¼ cup extra-virgin olive oil
- 2 pounds lobster meat (cooked)
- Lemon wedges (to garnish)
- Pita bread (to serve)

Directions:

1. Add the chickpea liquid to a mixing bowl along with the ice cubes. Set aside.

2. Add the drained chickpeas to a food processor followed by the garlic, freshly squeezed lemon juice, sea salt, and cumin. Process to fully combine.

3. Next, add the tahini and olive oil and at high speed, process.

4. Strain the chickpea liquid and gradually stream it into the processor until the hummus is pancake batter-like consistency.

5. When you are ready to serve, top with the lobster meat and garnish with wedges of lemon.

6. Serve with pita bread and enjoy.

vvvvvvvvvvvvvvvvvvvvvvvvvvvvvvvvvvvvvvvvvvvvvvvvvvvv

Chickpea-Free Flavors

vvvvvvvvvvvvvvvvvvvvvvvvvvvvvvvvvvvvvvvvvvvvvvvvvvv

Avocado and Zucchini Hummus

This hummus dip also works well spread in sandwiches or over grilled meats. It brings color, and depth of flavor to all number of dishes.

Servings: 12-16

Total Prep Time: 10mins

Ingredients:

- 2 medium zucchini
- 1 clove garlic (peeled, minced)
- ½ tsp ground cumin
- 2 tbsp freshly squeezed lemon juice
- 2 tbsp olive oil
- ¼ cup tahini
- 1 ripe avocado (peeled, pitted)
- 1 tsp sea salt

Toppings:

- 2 cups vine tomatoes (halved, chopped)
- Fresh cilantro (chopped)
- Olive oil (to drizzle)

Directions:

1. Slice the ends off each zucchini and cut into chunks. Aim to yield approximately 6 portions per zucchini.

2. Add the zucchini along with the garlic, ground cumin, lemon juice, olive oil, tahini, avocado and sea salt to a processor.

3. Process the ingredients until creamy, while scraping down the sides of the blender bowl or jug, a few times.

4. Set the blender to a high-speed setting and blend until ultra smooth. You can skip this step if you prefer a chunky consistency hummus.

5. Remove from the blender and enjoy topped with chopped tomatoes, fresh cilantro and a drizzle of olive oil.

vvvvvvvvvvvvvvvvvvvvvvvvvvvvvvvvvvvvvvvvvvvvvvvvvvvvv

Beet Hummus

As a veggie, beets are hugely under-rated, and this hummus dip is proof positive that they are totally versatile and tasty.

Servings: 12-16

Total Prep Time: 2hours 5mins

Ingredients:

- 1 pound beets (cooked, peeled, cooled)
- 3 tbsp tahini
- 1 garlic clove (peeled)
- 1 tbsp olive oil
- 3 tbsp freshly squeezed lemon juice
- 2 tsp ground cumin
- ½ tsp salt

Directions:

1. Cut the cooled beets into chunks and add to a food blender.

2. Add the tahini along with the garlic, olive oil, fresh lemon juice, ground cumin, and salt and process until entirely smooth. You may need to add additional oil until you achieve your preferred consistency.

3. Taste and season.

4. Cover and transfer to the fridge for 2-3 hours, to allow the flavor to develop.

5. Serve and enjoy.

vvvvvvvvvvvvvvvvvvvvvvvvvvvvvvvvvvvvvvvvvvvvvvvvvvvv

Buffalo Butternut Hummus

This dip goes a long way to making sure you and your family gets their 5-a-day.

Servings: 10-12

Total Prep Time: 40mins

Ingredients:

- 4 cups butternut squash cubes
- 1 tbsp avocado oil
- ½ cup store-bought buffalo wing sauce
- ½ cup tahini
- Veggie batons (to serve)

Directions:

1. Preheat the main oven to 350 degrees F.

2. Add the butternut squash to a bowl along with the olive oil and toss to coat.

3. Arrange the squash on a lined baking sheet.

4. Bake in the preheated oven until fork tender, for 20 minutes. Remove from oven and set aside to cool.

5. Add all the ingredients (cooled squash, buffalo wing sauce, and tahini) to a food processor and blend until creamy smooth.

6. Serve with veggie batons.

vvvvvvvvvvvvvvvvvvvvvvvvvvvvvvvvvvvvvvvvvvvvvvvvvvvvv

Butter Bean and Cumin Hummus

Just because you aren't a fan or chickpeas doesn't mean you can't tuck into a creamy dip and this recipe using butter beans has all the taste and flavor of traditional hummus.

Servings: 10-12

Total Prep Time: 20mins

Ingredients:

- 2 large-sized cloves of garlic (peeled)
- 2 (15 ounce) cans butter beans
- ⅔ cup tahini paste
- 6 tbsp freshly squeezed lemon juice
- ¼ cup extra-virgin olive oil
- 1 tbsp ground cumin
- 4-6 tbsp water (as needed)
- Salt and black pepper (to taste)

Directions:

1. In a food processor, chop the garlic finely.

2. Rinse and thoroughly drain the beans.

3. Next, add the butter beans along with the tahini, lemon juice, oil and cumin, and process until a smooth consistency.

4. One tablespoonful at a time, add the water until you achieve your desired consistency.

5. Season to taste with salt and black pepper.

6. Transfer to the fridge to chill before serving with pita or veggie batons.

vvvvvvvvvvvvvvvvvvvvvvvvvvvvvvvvvvvvvvvvvvvvvvvvvv

Cauliflower Hummus

Chickpea-free hummus is easy on the digestion, and this version using cauliflower is rich, creamy and super delicious.

Servings: 4

Total Prep Time: 1hour

Ingredients:

- 1 medium cauliflower (cut into florets)
- Olive oil
- ½ tsp salt (divided)
- 1 clove garlic (peeled)
- ⅓ cup tahini
- 3 tbsp freshly squeezed lemon juice
- Sunflower seeds (to garnish)
- Parsley (chopped, to serve)

Directions:

1. Add the florets to a large bowl along with 2 tbsp of olive oil and ¼ tsp of salt and toss to evenly coat.

2. Spread the florets out on a baking tray and bake in an oven set at 400 degrees F, for half an hour. You will need to stir the cauliflower after 15 minutes. Set aside to cool.

3. In a food processor, combine the cool cauliflower along with garlic, tahini, lemon juice, 2 tbsp of oil and ¼ tsp of salt, and blitz until creamy smooth. Taste and add additional oil, lemon juice or salt, as needed.

4. Transfer the mixture to a serving bowl and drizzle with oil.

5. Garnish with sunflower seeds and chopped parsley and serve.

vvvvvvvvvvvvvvvvvvvvvvvvvvvvvvvvvvvvvvvvvvvvvvvvvv

Edamame Hummus

Eat healthily with this protein and fiber-rich homemade hummus which switches chickpeas for edamame aka young soybeans in the pod.

Servings: 6

Total Prep Time: 5mins

Ingredients:

- 12 ounces frozen, shelled edamame
- 2 tbsp tahini
- 3 tbsp water
- 3 tbsp freshly squeezed lemon juice
- 4½ tbsp olive oil
- 1 garlic clove (peeled)
- 1 tsp cumin
- ½ tsp salt
- ½ tsp onion powder

Directions:

1. Cook the edamame according the package directions and set aside to cool.

2. Add the cooled edamame along with the tahini, water, lemon juice, oil, garlic, cumin, salt and onion powder to a food blender, and process to combine.

3. Transfer to the fridge until you are ready to serve.

Green Lentil Hummus

Gone to the pantry only to find that you are out of chickpeas?
No problem, lentils make a great hummus ingredient, too.

Servings: 6-8

Total Prep Time: 50mins

Ingredients:

- 1 cup dried green lentils
- 3 cups vegetable broth
- 2 cloves of garlic (peeled)
- ¼ cup olive oil
- ¼ cup tahini
- 2 tbsp freshly squeezed lemon juice
- 1 tsp ground cumin
- Salt (to taste)

Directions:

1. Mix the broth with the lentils in a pan over high heat and bring to boil.

2. Reduce the heat and uncovered, simmer for half an hour, or until the lentils are tender rather than mushy.

3. Drain, and return to the pan, allowing the lentil to completely cool, for 20-25 minutes.

4. Add the cooled lentils along with the garlic, oil, tahini, fresh lemon juice, cumin, and salt to a food processor and process until creamy smooth. You may need to scrape down the sides of the bowl as necessary.

5. Scrape the hummus into a serving bowl, drizzle with oil and serve.

vvvvvvvvvvvvvvvvvvvvvvvvvvvvvvvvvvvvvvvvvvvvvvvvvv

Lima Bean, Red Onion and Thyme Hummus

This hummus works well served on crostini along with crumbled goat cheese; successfully transforming a dip into a filling savory snack.

Servings: 8-10

Total Prep Time: 40mins

Ingredients:

- 16 ounces frozen lima beans
- Salted water
- 4 cloves garlic (peeled, roasted)
- Zest of 1 lemon
- Freshly squeezed juice of 3 lemons
- ¼ red onion (peeled, coarsely chopped)
- 2 tbsp thyme
- ¼ cup olive oil
- Salt and black pepper (to taste)
- Crostini (to serve, optional)
- Goat cheese (crumbled, to serve, optional)

Directions:

1. Cook the lima beans in salted water and according to the package instructions until tender, thoroughly drain.

2. Add the drained beans along with the roasted garlic, lemon zest, lemon juice, red onion, thyme, and oil to a food processor and process until smooth.

3. Taste, season and serve on crostini topped with crumbled goat cheese.

vvvvvvvvvvvvvvvvvvvvvvvvvvvvvvvvvvvvvvvvvvvvvvvvvv

Loaded Mexican Hummus

Hummus heads south of the border with this loaded spicy Mexican-inspired hummus.

Servings: 8-10

Total Prep Time: 10mins

Ingredients:

- 2 cups black beans (rinsed, divided)
- ¼ cup tahini
- 3 tbsp extra-virgin olive oil
- 2 cloves of garlic (peeled, minced)
- 1 tbsp hot sauce
- 2 tbsp freshly squeezed lime juice
- ½ tsp cumin
- ½ tsp salt

Toppings:

- ¼ cup red onions (peeled, finely diced)
- ¼ cup tomato (diced)
- ⅛ cup cilantro (chopped)
- 1 tbsp cotija cheese (crumbled)
- ¼ tsp sea salt
- 1 tbsp rice vinegar

Directions:

1. Add ½ cup of rinsed black beans to a bowl and set to one side.

2. Place the remaining 1½ cups of black beans in a food processor together with the tahini, olive oil, garlic, hot sauce, fresh lime juice, cumin, and salt. On high speed, blend. Scrape down the sides of the bowl as needed and add additional olive oil to thin out the consistency if necessary.

3. Pour the mixture over the black beans in the bowl, set aside earlier.

4. For the topping: In a bowl, combine the red onions with the tomato, chopped cilantro, and crumbled cheese. Season with salt and rice vinegar and scatter over the hummus.

5. Serve and enjoy.

vvvvvvvvvvvvvvvvvvvvvvvvvvvvvvvvvvvvvvvvvvvvvvvvvvvv

Zucchini Hummus

Made without chickpeas, this zucchini hummus tastes equally as good, and what's more, it's great for the digestion too.

Servings: 8-10

Total Prep Time: 7mins

Ingredients:

- 2 zucchini (peeled, chopped)
- ½ cup freshly squeezed lemon juice
- 2 garlic cloves (peeled)
- ¼ cup olive oil
- ⅔ cup tahini
- 1 tsp ground cumin
- 1 tsp salt

Directions:

1. Add the zucchini, lemon juice, garlic, oil, tahini, ground cumin and salt to a food blender and process until creamy smooth.

2. Set aside, to thicken.

3. Taste, and season before serving with crackers.

vvvvvvvvvvvvvvvvvvvvvvvvvvvvvvvvvvvvvvvvvvvvvvvv

Author's Afterthoughts

thank you

I would like to express my deepest thanks to you, the reader, for making this investment in one my books. I cherish the thought of bringing the love of cooking into your home.

With so much choice out there, I am grateful you decided to Purch this book and read it from beginning to end.

Please let me know by submitting an Amazon review if you enjoyed this book and found it contained valuable information to help you in your culinary endeavors. Please take a few minutes to express your opinion freely and honestly. This will help others make an informed decision on purchasing and provide me with valuable feedback.

Thank you for taking the time to review!

Christina Tosch

About the Author

Christina Tosch is a successful chef and renowned cookbook author from Long Grove, Illinois. She majored in Liberal Arts at Trinity International University and decided to pursue her passion of cooking when she applied to the world renowned Le Cordon Bleu culinary school in Paris, France. The school was lucky to recognize the immense talent of this chef and she excelled in her courses, particularly Haute Cuisine. This skill was recognized and rewarded by several highly regarded Chicago restaurants, where she was offered the prestigious position of head chef.

Christina and her family live in a spacious home in the Chicago area and she loves to grow her own vegetables and herbs in the garden she lovingly cultivates on her sprawling estate. Her and her husband have two beautiful children, 3 cats, 2 dogs and a parakeet they call Jasper. When Christina is not hard at work creating beautiful meals for Chicago's elite, she is hard at work writing engaging e-books of which she has sold over 1500.

Make sure to keep an eye out for her latest books that offer helpful tips, clear instructions and witty anecdotes that will bring a smile to your face as you read!

Printed in Great Britain
by Amazon